The English Channel

Robert Brustein

A SAMUEL FRENCH ACTING EDITION

SAMUEL FRENCH

FOUNDED 1830

SAMUELFRENCH.COM
SAMUELFRENCH-LONDON.CO.UK

THE ENGLISH CHANNEL was first produced by the Suffolk University Marilyn Plotkins, Artistic Director) and the Vineyard Playhouse (M.J. Munafo, Artistic Director), at the C. Walsh Theatre and the Vineyard Playhouse in 2007, and then at the Abingdon Theatre (Jan Buttram, Artistic Director) in New York.

The Boston performance was directed by Wesley Savick, with sets by Richard Chambers, costumes by costume designer, etc, etc. The Production Stage Manager was stage manager. The Boston and Vineyard cast was as follows:

WILLIAM SHAKESPEARE . . . . Gabriel Field

CHRISTOPHER MARLOWE . . . . .Sean Dugan

HENRY (HAL) WRIOTHESLEY,
    THIRD EARL OF SOUTHAMPTON . . . . Alex Pollock

EMILIA LANIER . . . . .Merritt Janson

The New York performance was directed by Daniela Varon, with sets and lighting by Mike Billings, costumes by Laura Crow, sound and music by Scott Killian. The production stage manager was Rebecca L. Hurlbert and the fight choreographer was Stafford Clark-Price. The New York cast was as follows:

WILLIAM SHAKESPEARE . . . . Stafford Clark-Price

CHRISTOPHER MARLOWE . . . . Sean Dugan

HENRY (HAL) WRIOTHESELY,
    THIRD EARL OF SOUTHAMPTON . . . . Brian Robert Burns

EMILIA LANIER . . . . Lori Gardner

CHARACTERS

WILLIAM SHAKESPEARE (WILL) – 29

**HENRY (HAL) WRIOTHESLEY (PRONOUNCED "RIZLEY"),
EARL OF SOUTHAMPTON – 19**

CHRISTOPHER MARLOWE (KIT) – 29

EMILIA LANIER – 23

SETTING

A room in the Mermaid Tavern

TIME

The plague year, 1953

PROLOGUE

MARLOWE'S GHOST. List, list! Oh, list!
I am the ghost of Christopher Marlowe;
Doomed for a certain term to walk the night,
And for the day confined to fast in fires...
(*breaks off*) Belike you've heard those doleful lines before?
You'll hear them oft again in future times,
The meek Will Shakespeare always put great store
In tarting up my brave iambic rhymes.
Poor poets borrow, greater poets steal,
We all gulp down the same embezzled meal,
But here's the question for your teeth to gnaw at:
Is Will a poetaster, or a poet?
At his fresh age, the answer still is moot,
His seeded fame has not yet taken root,
This errant husband, wayward father, swain,
This bashful yokel, pockets full of grain,
Who leaves his wife, his friends, his babes, his chattel,
To lock himself in fever'sh daily battle
With London's greatest playwrights, poets too,
Reviled and envied by the baser few.
Condemned for now to strut upon the stage,
Or alter and amend another's page,
Or squat at table, cramped in small, dark rooms-
Like this one where our present action looms....

(Lights up on **WILL** *writing on a table in a private room in the tavern. He is twenty-nine, looking like the Grafton*

portrait, with the trace of a moustache, a wispy beard, and a ring in his left ear. A palette bed. An Elizabethan armchair. A cabinet. On the wall a cross. Many theatre props, including halberds, broadswords, farthingales, buskins, doublets, hose, crowns, armor, and the like, piled around the room.)

MARLOWE'S GHOST. Let's watch our bending scrivener scribbling here.

It's 1593, a plague-filled year,

The place a stews, yclept the Mermaid Tavern,

Which Keats will liken to a mossy cavern.

I won't be dead until the end of May.

Till then, I'll be a person in this play.

(Exit)

ACT I

WILL. *(reading)* "Is it for fear to wet a widow's eye, That thou consum'st thyself in single life?"

(blots the page)

There's for the coupling. And here's for the tripling.

(writing)

"Look in thy glass, and tell the face thou viewest Now is the time that face should form another." Aye, that hits it, if rhyming can. Marriage, copulation, and birth.

*(Enter **HENRY WRIOTHESLEY**, the third **EARL OF SOUTHAMPTON**, a beautiful slender lad of nineteen with long flowing hair in ringlets, a double earring, painted cheeks and lips, and heavy-lidded eyes. He is waving a sheaf of papers in his hands in mock agitation.)*

SOUTHAMPTON. Master Shakespeare?

WILL. *(rising in agitation)* Your Lordship.

SOUTHAMPTON. You are Master William Shakespeare?

WILL. I am that man, my Lord.

SOUTHAMPTON. I looked for you in Shoreditch. They told me you'd be here.

WILL. My rooms in Shoreditch are contaminate.

SOUTHAMPTON. Like all of London. You make a smaller figure without your paint, your wig, your buskins.

WILL. You have seen me on the stage?

SOUTHAMPTON. Aye, and more than once, though ask not me the plays. I have no memory of diversion once I leave the playhouse. I use it only as a pastime.

WILL. I, too, prefer the purer world of poesy.

SOUTHAMPTON. By constraint I dare say, now that plague has closed the Theatre.

(looking over the costumes and properties in the room) I suppose the padlocked playhouses account for all this paraphernalia.

WILL. Indeed, sir, our manager has requested me to store these properties in my room.

SOUTHAMPTON. You know my secret longing? To play a monarch on the stage.

(putting a crown on his head, he picks up a mirror and examines himself.) "Is it not passing brave to be a King, and ride in triumph through Persepolis?"

WILL. *(not wild about the references to Tamburlaine)* You know well your Marlowe. But should your Lordship be abroad in such a rank, polluted time?

SOUTHAMPTON. *(placing the crown on a hook and trying on a cloak)* I am too young to dread impending death, too rash to fear its sting. I admire impetuous Tamburlaine, the Scythian shepherd who dared to burn the holy Koran…

WILL. "…and set black streamers in the firmament to signify the slaughter of the gods." I know the play, my Lord.

SOUTHAMPTON. 'Tis good you frequent rival theatres. Poets have much to teach each other. Well, to the matter. You are the author of these verses in my hand?

WILL. *(shyly)* May I see those papers, Lord?

SOUTHAMPTON. *(brusquely thrusting them at him)* I am amazed you haven't seen them, stuck as they are on every tree in Saint James Park.

WILL. I grieve to hear that, my Lord. They were penned for your eyes only.

SOUTHAMPTON. For mine? You know me then?

WILL. All the world does know you, sir. Your name and fame are legendary. But you and I have never met.

SOUTHAMPTON. Then why do you instruct me in my private life, as if you were my tutor.

WILL. Your tutor?

SOUTHAMPTON. On the subject of marrying and having children. *(reads)*
"Die single, and thine image dies with thee." "Make thee another self, for love of me." "But were some child of yours alive that time, You should live twice, in it and in my time."

WILL. *(looking over his shoulder and correcting)* That's "in my rime."

SOUTHAMPTON. Infernal impudence!

WILL. Your Lordship, a thousand pardons.

SOUTHAMPTON. Rime, time, who gives a damn.

WILL. I had hoped to present you my poor poems in person when the sequence was complete. Those lines were never writ for public eyes.

SOUTHAMPTON. They are being strewn throughout the city, making me a mockery to the common view.

WILL. But you are nowhere named, sir.

SOUTHAMPTON. But everywhere described. What know you of my life and loves? And why do you urge on me to generate a child? I'm not yet twenty.

WILL. I know, My Lord, but your guardian Lord Burghley…

SOUTHAMPTON. You mean my guard dog Burghley.

WILL. …is much concerned about your single state.

SOUTHAMPTON. It does not much surprise me. Lord Burghley, my guard dog, would have me marry his granddaughter, thus marry my fortune, and guard dog that as well.

WILL. Ah, that explains his haste to commission my poems.

SOUTHAMPTON. Under commission, are you? How much is he paying?

WILL. Sixpence a sonnet.

SOUTHAMPTON. That much.

(**SHAKESPEARE** *winces.*)

And how many of these bedding and begetting jingles have you written?

WILL. Thus far seventeen, my Lord.

SOUTHAMPTON. I'll give you a shilling a sonnet to change the subject.

WILL. To what?

SOUTHAMPTON. Your choice. God. The Fall of Man. My almond-colored eyes.

WILL. That would be an honor, sir.

SOUTHAMPTON. And five pounds more when you finish the project.

WILL. *(amazed)* You are more than generous, Lord.

SOUTHAMPTON. But blot out these imputations that I waste my seed upon the ground, hear?

WILL. What?

SOUTHAMPTON. *(reading)* "Why dost thou spend upon thyself thy beauty's legacy?… Do not traffic with thyself alone." What should that mean else but self-abuse, that I am having a honeymoon in the hand?

WILL. Mere metaphor, my Lord, in the hortatory mode. But, truly, do I have your lordship's leave to draw your golden countenance in tables of ravishment?

SOUTHAMPTON. You do.

WILL. Then mine brush will celebrate your beauty for all time.

SOUTHAMPTON. I expect you to flatter me. It is the convention. So did Petrarch his Laura and Sidney his Stella.

WILL. Not flattery, my Lord. One cannot offer more than this rich praise, that you alone are you. Hum. That could be something. *(stops to write this down)*

SOUTHAMPTON. Good start. Here's a shilling.

WILL. I am most grateful, my Lord. *(eagerly)* With your leave, Right Honorable, may I broach another subject?

SOUTHAMPTON. Broach away.

WILL. I have a long poem completed, Venus and Adonis, based on Ovid. May I dedicate this, the first heir of my invention, to your Lordship? I would account myself most richly graced.

SOUTHAMPTON. Why not? Like Adonis, I have been pursued by older women.

WILL. And so indeed have I.

SOUTHAMPTON. My library at Titchfield contains three rare editions of Ovid. You must visit me there.

WILL. A private library! I am sore in need of reading matter.

SOUTHAMPTON. For pastime?

WILL. No for stories. I am needful of invented tales.

SOUTHAMPTON. I sense you also need a well-heeled patron.

WILL. I do, my Lord, though I fear to ask so strong a prop to support so weak a burden.

SOUTHAMPTON. Nicely said. You'll no doubt want some cash.

WILL. Whatever your Lordship thinks appropriate.

SOUTHAMPTON. For quills and paper, no?

WILL. I hope some day to have the means to buy a share in our acting company.

SOUTHAMPTON. How much would that take?

WILL. Fifty pounds.

SOUTHAMPTON. Here is ten pounds towards that distant day. Since you are a fountain of rhyme, I must be a wellspring of currency. But whence comes this torrent of sonnets. I thought you a mere player.

WILL. I am, my Lord.

SOUTHAMPTON. And yet a sonneteer?

WILL. Yes, and also sometimes a maker of plays.

SOUTHAMPTON. Ah, so that's why you need those stories.

WILL. Yes, my Lord. My persons are my own. My plots I borrow from others.

SOUTHAMPTON. I remember me now, you wrote those histories of Henry VI.

WILL. *(flattered)* Indeed, I did, sir.

SOUTHAMPTON. And whence came they?

WILL. From the chronicles of Holinshed.

SOUTHAMPTON. I would have guessed from the epics of Marlowe. Your Henrys much resemble Tamburlaine.

WILL. *(dashed)* How so, my Lord?

SOUTHAMPTON. A two-part vaulting history, composed in unrhymed five-stress ten-syllable iambics?

WILL. *(defensive)* I have written a third part. And am framing a fourth.

SOUTHAMPTON. Good, then there's hope some day you may outreach the famous Overreacher himself.

WILL. Your Lordship's knowledge of Marlowe's writing continues to impress me.

SOUTHAMPTON. I learned prosody at the age of twelve at St. John's College, Cambridge, from the poet himself. It was the author of Doctor Faustus who taught me how to scan a verse…

WILL. Indeed!

SOUTHAMPTON. …and cut a purse.

WILL. A cutpurse? You!

SOUTHAMPTON. I was the decoy, he the thief. That's how Marlowe kept his brain awake when his Muse was nodding.

*(The door bursts open and **CHRISTOPHER MARLOWE** enters, carrying a book, which he throws upon the table.)*

MARLOWE. I thought I'd find you at the Mermaid here, dodging those dodgy corpses in the street. Have you seen this slanderous piece of…. *(peering at* **SOUTHAMPTON***)* Now who is *this* comely youth?

SOUTHAMPTON. You do not know me?

MARLOWE. The eyes I know.

SOUTHAMPTON. Henry Wriothesley. The boy that you called Hal.

MARLOWE. By heaven, the boy that I called Hal. And nearer to heaventhan when I saw him last. My gamesome Hal. My captivating Helen.

WILL. What?

MARLOWE. This lad played Helen of Troy when Faustus was first performed at Cambridge. Age…what? Thirteen? And such a beauty! "Was this the face that launched a thousand ships….? Sweet Helen, make me immortal with a kiss."

(And he kisses SOUTHAMPTON *full on the mouth.* SOUTHAMPTON *returns it.* SHAKESPEARE *looks on in astonishment.)*

MARLOWE. What are you gaping at? Those are fools who love not tobacco and boys.

SOUTHAMPTON. No more a boy, Kit. I'll soon be twenty.

MARLOWE. Old enough to have a boy of your own, I'll warrant.

WILL. Indeed, Lord Burghley has been strongly urging him to marry and make an heir.

MARLOWE. *(wryly)* That's not what I meant. *(to* SOUTHAMPTON*)* So what are you up to, Hal? Still accomplicing cutpurses?

SOUTHAMPTON. I have advanced beyond that subtle art you taught me.

MARLOWE. So I hear. Rumor has you plotting rebellion with the malcontent Essex. Stay far from him. He is born to trouble, as the sparks fly upwards.

SOUTHAMPTON. Well, rumor has you a government spy in the pay of the Queen.

MARLOWE. Rumor is a false wench, who would paint libels on a saint. No, I'm just a penurious poet, finishing off his latest play. Which will amaze the world once they reopen those pest-ridden playhouses.

WILL. And the title?

MARLOWE. The Massacre at Paris. Guise and the French Catholics slaughter all the Protestant Huegenots. Delicious carnage. Gouts and gouts of blood.

WILL. Why stir up strife against the Catholics, Kit? Recusants suffer too much as it is.

MARLOWE. So long as the action swells and rouses, Will. Catholic, Protestant, Anabaptist or Puritan, it's all the same mendacity. Christianity's a fraud –

WILL. Lower your voice.

MARLOWE. …Jesus was a bastard –

WILL. Shhh!

MARLOWE. …and his mother was a whore.

WILL. Kit, that's damned heresy!

MARLOWE. And John the Evangelist used Christ as did the sinners of Sodom.

WILL. A capital offense.

MARLOWE. So are buggery and sorcery, both of which I practice.

SOUTHAMPTON. Under protection of the Queen's Protestant piety.

MARLOWE. What mean you?

SOUTHAMPTON. She has not recruited you to sniff out Catholics?

MARLOWE. That's a lie!

SOUTHAMPTON. And placed you in the employ of her spymaster, the malformed Robert Cecil?

MARLOWE. Another damnable lie!

SOUTHAMPTON. Well, lay the blame on that painted wench, Rumor. I must go.

MARLOWE. So soon, Hal? I long to hear how have you fared since your father's death? Is your mother still alive? Is she still succoring Papist priests?

(He pronounces this with the emphasis on "suck.")

SOUTHAMPTON. I no longer see the wretched woman. And who inquires after Papist priests? My friend? Or the Queen's ear?

MARLOWE. Your friend, Hal, your friend. Forever your friend.

SOUTHAMPTON. My business here is done. Until next week, Master Shakespeare, when I expect a dozen fresh new sonnets in my hand.

WILL. I will not sleep until that day, your Lordship. I will write until my fingers bleed.

SOUTHAMPTON. And you hear? No more about matrimony and parenthood. *(to **MARLOWE**)* Farewell, Kit. We will meet again.

MARLOWE. You will not stay the night, and join your old teacher in snatching a few purses? 'Tis an easy practice now the Watch is shunning the streets.

SOUTHAMPTON. Who, I rob? I a thief? Not I, by my faith.

MARLOWE. Then farewell to you, Hal, my heart, my bountiful boy.

(**SOUTHAMPTON** *exits. To **WILL**:)*

Have you done him yet?

WILL. Done what?

MARLOWE. Made him your bumboy. He's always had the roundest rump in Christendom. When still a stripling, he was my model for Ganymede, Jupiter's cupbearing catamite. Is he your cupbearer?

WILL. He is my new patron, for whom I feel a ripening friendship. More like my Damon.

MARLOWE. You mean your Pyth-i-ass.

WILL. The warm regard I feel for him resembles more that perfect love idealized by the Greek philosophers.

MARLOWE. Plato's ideal love was paederastice and Socrates was forced to swallow hemlock juice for buggering schoolboys. *(He is looking over **WILL**'s writings.)*

WILL. Nay, ideal love is innocent and pure.

MARLOWE. You call this pure, this panegyric to a male paramour?

*(picking up one of **WILL**'s verses)*

WILL. Don't touch that!

MARLOWE. *(ignoring him, and holding the verse away as* **WILL** *tries to snatch it)* "A woman's face with Nature's own hand painted Hast thou, the master-mistress of my passion...."

Master-mistress! That is hot ice and black snow. And who could be the inspiration for this oxymoronic androgyny? Hal?

WILL. *(blushing)* In my imagination–

MARLOWE. *(continuing to read)* "A woman's gentle heart, but not acquainted With shifting change, as is false woman's fashion..." Sounds like buggery to me.

WILL. Poetic license –

MARLOWE. Poetic licentiousness. Your tongue speaks ideal love, but your pistol is cocked for action.

WILL. The poem merely confirms the Earl a courteous and exquisite gentleman...

(He puts this and his other sonnets into his closet and locks it.)

MARLOWE. And full of game, I'll testify.

WILL. ...a fresh and delicate young courtier. Well worthy of an honest woman's love.

MARLOWE. And why not a man's? Don't reverence love, you animal, don't reverence love. It is but a lust of the blood and a permission of the will.

WILL. Hum. That could be something.*(He writes it down.)*

MARLOWE. Still ransacking my ship of verse, you poet-pirate?

WILL. What?

MARLOWE. My lines. My personages. My plays. You've filched enough of my lines to persuade the world you're an imposter – a Stratford bumpkin impersonating the great Kit Marlowe, or the great Kit Marlowe masquerading as a Stratford bumpkin. Next they'll be whispering you did not write your plays.

WILL. Who wrote them then?

MARLOWE. Why, any fool with a foolish piece of foolscap. *(laughing)* Oxford. Bacon. Me.

WILL. You?

MARLOWE. Which reminds me, have you seen this? *(picks up the book he threw on the table).*

WILL. What?

MARLOWE. Bob Greene's Groatsworth of Wit.

WILL. A bad poet, a worse playwright.

MARLOWE. He's on his deathbed, fighting for breath and defaming his betters. He calls me atheist, which I freely confess, and "a famous gracer of tragedians," which I would confess did I understand the meaning. What he says of you will wait until we've had that perfect potion for this pesky pestilence, a pot of ale. *(calling)* Francis!!

VOICE. Yes, sir.

MARLOWE. Two pints for me and one more for my friend.

VOICE. Anon, anon, sir!

MARLOWE. Anon, anon, sir. That means next Wednesday. Regarding you, Master William Shakespeare, Master Greene, that decomposing sack of compost, inscribes the following: *(reading)* "For there is an upstart crow, beautified with our feathers, that in his tiger's heart wrapped in a player's hide...

WILL. "Wrapped in a woman's hide!" That line he stole from my Henrys. And "beautified" is an ill phrase, a vile phrase.

MARLOWE. May I continue? "...this upstart crow...

WILL. You don't have to repeat it!

MARLOWE. "...supposes he is as well able to bombast out a blank verse as the best of you, and is in his own conceit the only Shakescene in the country."

*(**SHAKESPEARE** groans.)*

Confess it. Is there not a grainsworth of truth buried in this groatsworth of shit? Do you not steal?

WILL. Who asks? Kit the cutpurse?

MARLOWE. No, Marlowe the Magnificent.

WILL. I do not well understand this envious malice. An upstart crow?

MARLOWE. Meaning one cannot write a proper line of blank verse without a sound classical education.

WILL. I have a sound classical education.

MARLOWE. Ben Jonson, himself an uneducated son of a bricklayer, has been overheard to say you have small Latin and less Greek.

WILL. Another envious man.

MARLOWE. And do you not envy your betters? Next they'll be whispering you did not write your plays.

WILL. Who wrote them then?

MARLOWE. Why, any fool with a foolish piece of foolscap.

(laughing)

Oxford. Bacon. Me.

WILL. You?

MARLOWE. Are we not two peas in a peascod? Am I not your better-educated, more capable duplicate? I am twenty-nine, and you are…?

WILL. Twenty-nine.

MARLOWE. I a cobbler's son, you a… What was your father, then?

WILL. A glover.

MARLOWE. A glover.

WILL. And later a wool dealer.

MARLOWE. Which explains your weakness for woolgathering. A wool dealer, you say? A prosperous trade. Why did he not send you to university?

WILL. Marriage was my university. I entered that stifling cloister at age eighteen with a bride of twenty-six.

MARLOWE. And a bun in the oven, I'll warrant, before the marriage meats were warm?

WILL. A baby girl, yes, three months on the way.

MARLOWE. An o'erhasty marriage followed by a swift retreat to London to seek your fortune on the stage. What is the name of this seductress, I wonder?

WILL. Ann Hathaway.

MARLOWE. Of course. You had your will but Ann hath her way.

WILL. *(bitter)* I was a boy, hot for any wench who'd have me. This one did. In a cornfield. I ploughed her, and she cropped.

MARLOWE. And now she sits in Stratford, like patient Griselda, waiting for Wandering Will to return to his deserted wife and abandoned child.

WILL. Children, actually. After Susannah, we had twins. Hamnet and Judith.

MARLOWE. Hamnet. Is that not a Danish name?

WILL. Not that I know.

MARLOWE. A prince in Saxo Grammaticus whose uncle kills his father and marries his mother.

WILL. Not a bad idea for a play.

MARLOWE. No, I'm thinking of Hamlet. It has been written. Didn't you know? By my chamber-mate Thom Kyd.

WILL. All the great stories are already told.

MARLOWE. That's why you steal, dear Will. That's why you steal.

(Knock at the door. **MARLOWE** *opens it, and comes back with three pots of ale.)*

MARLOWE. Here we are. A harmony of hops and malt.

(He downs two pots in two gulps. **SHAKESPEARE** *sips at his.)*

So, Will is alone in plague-ridden London, his theatre closed, his occupation gone, unwived, unwomaned, and unwanted. That condition must be changed, and swiftly, too. Let me see. I have it. There is a lady presently at court, her name Emilia Lanier, that is as lovely as a night in May. Jet-black hair, onyx eyes, olive skin. If I weren't a confirmed sodomite, I would thump her myself.

WILL. And she's unmarried?

MARLOWE. No, there's the thing. She was the mistress of Lord Hunsdon, a patron of your company, no? She conceived a child by him, though he was old enough to be her grandsire. And so he married her off to Alfonso Lanier, a musician, providing him a large pension, a basketful of jewels, and a big-bellied wife.

WILL. She belongs to another, then.

MARLOWE. Why, so do you, man, so do you. Her husband cares not whom she beds so long as he can fish for trout in other waters.

WILL. And she is dark.

MARLOWE. If hairs be wires, black wires grow on her head. But I think you'll find her lovely beyond compare. (**WILL** *is writing.*) Stop writing, damn you!

WILL. What is her breeding?

MARLOWE. She has none. The bastard daughter of a convert Jew of Venice. Shall I bring her to you? You'll never want another woman.

WILL. A Jewess of Venice, pandered by the man who wrote The Jew of Malta?

MARLOWE. She is a lot more desirable than Barabas, I assure you.

WILL. She doesn't poison wells or kill sick people groaning under walls?

MARLOWE. Poetic license, as you say, Will. Poetic license.

WILL. That character was excessive, Kit. I think were I to write a Jew…

MARLOWE. And you will, Master Shakescene, you will.

WILL. …he would have some saving grace, whate'er his savage nature.

MARLOWE. Would he also have a beautiful daughter who turns Christian and runs off with a poet? I can provide the model.

WILL. Bring her then. And I will stain my marriage bed again.

MARLOWE. *(going)* One thing more. I have penned a poem that wants a patron. You may guess I intend to solicit Hal. He has pockets deep enough for both of us.

WILL. *(dashed)* I cannot stop you. But you accuse me of stealing. I s not that a kind of theft as well?

MARLOWE. Not a worry, Will. I will bring you back a prize worth all the Earl's revénue.

*(***MARLOWE*** *exits, lights dim to suggest a passage of time and he returns immediately with* **EMILIA LANIER**, *twenty-three years old, as dark and beautiful as she was described.)*

ACT II

MARLOWE. And here she is. Sir Troilus, prepare to meet your Cressida.

(**WILL** *rises from his chair. He and* **EMILIA** *look at each other. Long pause.*)

EMILIA. I blush, Master Shakespeare, at the fulfillment of a deep desire. I have long longed to meet the man who wrote Titus Andronicus. He is poised to become an immortal English playwright.

WILL. Where did you find this shrewd judicious lady? I discover myself of a sudden strangely drawn to her.

MARLOWE. Of course you are, man. Whoever loved that loved not at first sight, as another immortal playwright wrote. Me, of course.

WILL. An immortal who wants to steal my patron?

MARLOWE. An immortal who needs to have a drink. *(calls out)* Francis!! Fetch me a cup of canary.

FRANCIS. *(off)* Anon, anon, sir.

MARLOWE. That means next Shrovetide. Well, I will leave you together for closer acquaintance, whilst I prevail upon the tapster below to draw that heady brew. Farewell, Emilia, till we meet again at court. *(slaps her on the rump and leaves)*

EMILIA. A perplexing man, Kit Marlowe. That such an aspiring mind could companion such a paltry spirit.

WILL. Another spirit inhabits him, a rash and dangerous thing I do not understand.

EMILIA. Know you he was charged with murder once and sent to Newgate?

WILL. Kit in prison?

EMILIA. They held him two weeks, and released him. He has powerful friends.

WILL. Kit is too familiar with the murderous Machiavel and other such Italian villains. *(embarrassed pause)* I am told there is Italian blood in you.

EMILIA. My late father was Baptista Bassano.

WILL. *(writing)* Baptista. Bassano. Good names for a play.

EMILIA. Perhaps you knew of him? A Venetian famous for the viol de gambol in the court of our late King Henry. I myself do play recorder for the Queen.

WILL. And that explains the music of your voice.

EMILIA. *(mock curtsey)* Why thank you, la.

WILL. Wilt play for me?

EMILIA. With pleasure Master Shakespeare. *(And she plays "Hey ho, the wind and the rain.")*

WILL. Most lovely. With your sweet fingers, you make dead wood more blest than living lips.

EMILIA. And your sweet lips make language blessed, too.

WILL. I hear no trace of Italy in your speech.

EMILIA. I was a babe when Father brought me to these shores.

(beat)

WILL. Kit tells me Lord Hunsdon was your friend.

EMILIA. My protector…

WILL. Yes.

EMILIA. …and the father of my daughter. Though fifty years my senior.

WILL. *(embarrassed at her frankness)* I see.

EMILIA. Yes, my daughter is a bastard, and the daughter of a bastard. But Lord Hunsdon has been kind to me. He brought me to your plays.

WILL. You are a lover of the theatre?

EMILIA. Of the persons that you write.

WILL. I love them, too, when they do not crowd me from the room.

EMILIA. What mean you?

WILL. Sometimes they make demands on me that drain my strength.

EMILIA. You speak as one who does not command his creations.

WILL. I am more their hostage than their host.

EMILIA. But yet their sole begetter.

WILL. Better say their conduit, their passage to the outside world. At times they come to me when I'm asleep, sometimes when I lie sleepless, demanding entry. Their hungry voices clamoring in my ear, they plead for life. And once I give them life, they plead for greater life.

EMILIA. What kind of life?

WILL. Oh, that I correct their meter, improve their speech, enlarge their parts, as if they were my fellow actors on the stage. I have no rest or peace from their entreaties.

EMILIA. They are well worth your sleeplessness.

WILL. *(flattered)* You think so? And which of them do you fancy most?

EMILIA. Why, Katherina, your Paduan shrew. I love her spirit and her wit. Though sad I was to see her bending at the end.

WILL. Ah, perhaps that surrender was but feigned, and she has won the victory after all.

EMILIA. How well you know our weaknesses and strengths. Not Chapman, not Lyly, and certainly not Marlowe can match your knowledge of the female heart.

WILL. I thank you, but no one truly knows a woman's heart.

EMILIA. I'll be your instructor, beginning with a lesson in anatomy.

(She puts his hand upon her breast.)

WILL. That hemisphere is rounded, full, and temperate. I'll try its twin to test the symmetry.

(WILL puts his hand on the other breast.)

EMILIA. I see you're familiar with the Northern countries.

WILL. I would explore the nether regions, too. So, patiently and yielding…

(They go into a deep kiss.)

You have witchcraft in your lips.

(The lights fade for a moment. When they go on again, EMILIA is lying on the palette bed, naked from the waist up, and WILL is writing at his desk, wiping his forehead with an embroidered handkerchief with strawberries on it.)

EMILIA. Where is my lover? Why is he a stranger to my bed?

WILL. I am a native of every nation in your body.

EMILIA. Nay, there are territories still left unexplored.

WILL. Some later time. The desire may be boundless, but the act is slave to limit.

EMILIA. Most lovers swear more performance than they are able. But you promise less. Come back to bed, if but to sleep.

WILL. I am at my table, my love, composing a sonnet stirred by you.

EMILIA. Read it me.

WILL. You will not like it.

EMILIA. Try me anyway.

WILL. "My mistress' eyes are nothing like the sun; Coral is far more red than her lips' red; If snow be white, why then her breasts are dun; If hairs be wires, black wires grow on her head."

EMILIA. And that is praise?

WILL. Actually, Marlowe gave me the black wires. The rest is mine. "I have seen roses damask'd, red and white, But no such roses see I in her cheeks; And in some perfumes is there more delight Than in the breath that from my mistress reeks."

EMILIA. Will! My God!

WILL. "I love to hear her speak…"

EMILIA. At last! A compliment.

WILL. "…yet well I know That music hath a far more pleasing sound; I grant I never saw a goddess go; My mistress, when she walks, treads on the ground…"

EMILIA. And that's a love poem, Will? I have heard more fulsome panegyrics uttered to a horse.

WILL. Ah, but you haven't heard the final couplet: "And yet, by heaven, I think my love as rare As any she belied with false compare."

EMILIA. *(She rises from the bed to throw her arms around his shoulders.)* Don't compare women, sweet Will, and do not libel us neither. We endure enough slander from the mouths of men. I have written poetry about that subject myself. Would you care to hear a stanza?

WILL. I am working, fair Emilia. Perhaps a quatrain.

EMILIA. Why then, a couplet. *(Clears her throat)* "God bless my soul, why are poor women blamed, Or by more faulty men so much defamed." *(Nervous)* What do you think?

WILL. A bit doggerel-like, perhaps, but you make your case. Are all your verses written in defense of women?

EMILIA. Not all women.

WILL. Who are the exceptions?

EMILIA. Why, those forgetful they were born of women, nourished of women, who do like vipers deface the wombs wherein they breed.

WILL. 'Tis true that women first brought sin into the world.

EMILIA. And men who first traduced them to it. Will, you disappoint me. You repeat the same libels on our sex as I daily hear at court.

WILL. At court is where your sex is most exposed.

EMILIA. Do I hear a hint of woman-hatred in your tone? I imagined the author of Titus a more liberal man.

WILL. How so?

EMILIA. A poet who could imagine both the virtuous Lavinia and the lustful Queen Tamora?

WILL. Well, the world is peopled with the innocent and the impure. I am charged to give a voice to all.

EMILIA. And in which pigeonhole will you stuff me?

WILL. That will depend upon what bird you prove to be.

EMILIA. What kind of bird are you, that wears his wedding ring in his ear?

WILL. Why, one who listens for the cuckoo's call.

EMILIA. And has the cuckoo called to you?

WILL. My wife is far away. I visit her but once a year.

EMILIA. She is made of flesh like you. She has her appetites as well.

WILL. And what of wedding vows? Are those mere words?

(He is wiping his brow with the handkerchief.)

EMILIA. *(taking his handkerchief)* Is this your handkerchief? It is more like a woman's.

WILL. My mother gave it me.

EMILIA. I'll take it as a keepsake of this precious night.

WILL. Of which you've had a number, I would guess.

EMILIA. *(stung)* I am not your wife. For affection to grow, it must be nourished on courtesy.

WILL. I grant you that.

EMILIA. And honesty as well. You know I am married.

WILL. I do, Emilia.

EMILIA. And you are not my first lover.

WILL. I have guessed at that.

EMILIA. And may not be the last.

WILL. That thought has dawned on me as well.

EMILIA. And will that be a cause for pouring infamy on our sex?

(WILL is silent.)

EMILIA. This napkin I shall cherish. But let me leave some token in exchange. How like you this my instrument?

WILL. I liked it well enough last night.

EMILIA. Nay, naughty man, I speak of my recorder.

WILL. I cannot take that. It is your livelihood.

EMILIA. I have a dozen others.

WILL. I know not the stops.

EMILIA. 'Tis easy. Govern these ventages with your fingers and thumbs, give it breath with your mouth, and it will discourse most eloquent music.

WILL. *(tries a few notes)* I have not the feel of it.

EMILIA. I shall instruct you.

(From behind, she puts her arms around his arms and places his fingers on the stops.)

*(***SOUTHAMPTON*** comes bursting into the room.)*

SOUTHAMPTON. *(takes in the scene)* Good morning, Will. Do you teach this maid the rudiments of poetry?

WILL. *(Embarrassed, rising to his feet. She quickly covers her bosom.)* She is teaching me music.

SOUTHAMPTON. If music be the food of love, play on, and spare me indigestion.

WILL. My Lord Southampton, let me present Emilia Lanier, a lady of the court.

SOUTHAMPTON. *(as she curtsies to him)* I believe I have seen her there. Your dark beauty stands out among the fair.

EMILIA. And your young beauty stands out among the old.

SOUTHAMPTON. Did I not dance with you at Whitehall once?

EMILIA. You know right well you did.

SOUTHAMPTON. Indeed, I did.

EMILIA. How needless was it then to ask the question.

SOUTHAMPTON. You must not be so quick.

EMILIA. Because of you who prompt me with such questions.

SOUTHAMPTON. Your wit's too hot, it speeds too fast, 'twill tire.

EMILIA. Not till it leave the rider in the mire.

(**SHAKESPEARE** *is writing furiously all this while.*)

SOUTHAMPTON. She is a wit, your lady.

WILL. *(gloomily)* And a poet, too, my Lord.

SOUTHAMPTON. Which reminds me of my cause for coming. Have you penned me any sonnets yet?

WILL. Aye, a score or more.

SOUTHAMPTON. I owe the man two pounds. *(giving him the money)* You write like one possessed. Let me look at them.

EMILIA. My Lord, I should be going. I will see you soon at court, I trust. Adieu.

SOUTHAMPTON. God send you many lovers.

EMILIA. Amen, so you be none.

(A long look between them.)

EMILIA. Adieu, My Lord. Adieu, Will Shakespeare. Till our next encounter.

(**SHAKESPEARE** *barely nods goodbye. She leaves.*)

WILL. Here are the sonnets, my Lord *(handing him the poems, with a sour expression)*.

SOUTHAMPTON. What, chopfallen? Dejected by our idle banter?

WILL. She seemed to revel in the exchange.

SOUTHAMPTON. You expect too much of women. None are true except in poets' minds. *(reading)* Ahem, as you say here: "A woman's gentle heart, but not acquainted With shifting change, as is false woman's fashion…" Indeed, you are even less forgiving of the sex than I am.

WILL. That poem was written about you.

SOUTHAMPTON. Really? *(continuing)* "And for a woman wert thou first created; Till Nature as she wrought thee, fell adoting, And by addition me of thee defeated, By adding one thing to my purpose no-thing." What's that thing?

WILL. Read on.

SOUTHAMPTON. "But since she prick'd thee out for woman's pleasure, Mine be thy love, and thy love's use their treasure." Very flattering, Will, but Nature pricked me out for use by both the sexes.

WILL. 'Tis certain your countenance pleases both the sexes.

SOUTHAMPTON. I would it pleased the Queen.

WILL. How could it not?

SOUTHAMPTON. I have fallen out of favor with the ugly hag.

WILL. My lord, all English poets call her the divine Gloriana.

SOUTHAMPTON. *(passionately)* She is an irksome, hairless, toothless tyrant, whose mind is as crooked as her carcass. She murdered our rightful monarch Catholic Mary of Scotland, and imprisoned my father for four years in the Tower, along with anyone who dared to go to Mass. The Pope has excommunicated her, offering absolution to the man who kills her. I would I were that man.

WILL. My Lord, you know not whereof you speak.

SOUTHAMPTON. I know whereof I speak, and to whom. A secret recusant, no?

WILL. I am no wafer-eater, sir.

SOUTHAMPTON. But a believer like your father, are you not?

WILL. I believe in the power of poetry to breach the invisible borders of the imagination.

SOUTHAMPTON. Very pretty, Will, but you cannot be a neutral in this struggle. You will have to choose.

WILL. It is not my nature to join in broils of others making. Forgive me, Lord.

SOUTHAMPTON. Not even when your fellow religionists are strangling in a tyrant's choke-hold? I say she must be stopped.

WILL. Let us pray God that first the Queen come round.

SOUTHAMPTON. She will come round when first we force her round. Something too much of that. I came to say

I am much pleased with your Venus and Adonis. I felt myself not so much its patron as its hero.

WILL. And so you are its hero, dear my love. I mean my dearly loved Lord.

SOUTHAMPTON. You are a rare poet, Will. And you may call me "love."

WILL. You know I use the word in gratitude, for all I owe you for your liberal patronage. But I begin to fear my days are past the best.

SOUTHAMPTON. Why, man, you've not reached thirty yet.

WILL. I sense my feeble Muse is being overtaken by a stronger sail.

SOUTHAMPTON. You mean Kit Marlowe? Indeed, his Hero and Leander is a soaring piece of work.

WILL. Which makes my art seem tongue-tied, knowing a better spirit now does please you more.

SOUTHAMPTON. I know not how to choose between you as poets, Will, but you are sure the better spirit.

WILL. But none compares with you. There is more life in one of your fair eyes than any poet can in praise invoke. Yet not too long ago my Muse alone had all your kind attention.

SOUTHAMPTON. I am not married to your Muse, Will, however it doth service me. I have been the subject of some half dozen volumes of verse ere now.

WILL. I doubt it not. You well deserve the praise of worthier pens. And since not one alone can sum your quality, you have full rights to seek another stamp.

SOUTHAMPTOM. *(testy)* I know my rights, sir. And shall assert them, as I please.

WILL. My pardon, Lord, I meant you no offense.

SOUTHAMPTON. And none was taken.

WILL. If you hate me, I cannot love myself.

SOUTHAMPTON. It is forgotten, Will. Forgotten. Let's try a calmer subject. Tell me of Emilia.

WILL. This was our first night together. And though I feel most strangely drawn to her, I feel most strangely tainted, too.

SOUTHAMPTON. Tainted by what?

WILL. Betrayal.

SOUTHAMPTON. You are too ticklish, man. Learn to take your pleasures whence you can.

WILL. Even when those pleasures prove an expense of spirit in a waste of shame? Hum. That could be something.

(writing)

If you'll spare me a moment.

SOUTHAMPTON. I'll spare you a hundred, and take my leave. I have a meeting with Essex that may prove crucial to our cause.

WILL. Proceed with caution, my love. Your safety and your life are worth the world to me.

SOUTHAMPTON. To me as well. But I must go secure the right to practice my beliefs.

WILL. And I must stay to write the beauty of your countenance.

SOUTHAMPTON. I know, I know, and make me immortal in your rhymes. Farewell, Will.

(and swings out the door)

(**WILL** *returns to writing at the fade.*)

ACT III

(A few days later. Morning. **EMILIA** *in bed. Unfinished food upon the table.* **WILL** *pacing the room.)*

WILL. I tell you, I saw it.

EMILIA. I say you did not.

WILL. And I must doubt the evidence of my own eyes?

EMILIA. Believe what you will, I gave it no one.

WILL. Then deliver it me.

EMILIA. I cannot. I have it not about.

WILL. Not?

EMILIA. I think it lost.

WILL. Lost? The single relic of my mother's memory? The early token of our young and, it would seem, abortive love?

EMILIA. You must believe me, Will.

WILL. Even when you lie?

EMILIA. I only lie when you do not believe me.

WILL. How's that again? *(going to his table and taking up his pen)*

EMILIA. *(impatient)* Lay down your quill.

WILL. *(writing and speaking aloud)* "When my love swears that she is made of truth I do believe her though I know she lies..."

EMILIA. Will, you are making a poem...

WILL. "That she might think me some untutored youth, Unlearned in the world's false subtleties..."

EMILIA. ...but losing a lover.

WILL. The handkerchief. Fetch it, let me see it.

EMILIA. Your sonnets, are they pleasing to Hal?

WILL. The handkerchief.

EMILIA. I pray you, talk to me of Hal.

WILL. I do. I saw him wipe his lips with it.

EMILIA. The handkerchief again.

WILL. I say I saw it in his hand.

EMILIA. Some other handkerchief surely.

WILL. *(pulling her towards the bed, roughly)* No, mine, the thing I gave to you before you gave your thing to him.

EMILIA. My thing, as you so chivalrously call it, is not in your custody. If you claim ownership, where is the receipt?

WILL. Only strumpets put their bodies out for hire.

EMILIA. Only great ladies are independent of a lord's largesse.

WILL. What?

EMILIA. The blossoms of love are free. The soil that brings them forth cannot flower in fallow fields.

WILL. I am a poor poet.

EMILIA. I know that well. And one that cannot write without a patron.

WILL. You need a patron? You had Lord Hunsdon. Now you have your husband.

EMILIA. That one? A wastrel who squanders all his patrimony on whores?

I have a young daughter to support.

WILL. How much do I owe you for our nights in bed?

EMILIA. Have I asked for money?

WILL. Not yet.

EMILIA. Nor will I. But if you need a guarantee, I have lately been patronized by none but you.

WILL. And that's the truth?

EMILIA. That is a kind of truth.

WILL. *(smiling and pulling her towards the bed)* And so I lie with her, and she with me, and in our faults by lies we flattered be.

EMILIA. *(getting up and getting dressed)* I'll not lie with you, Will Shakespeare. Not till you cease your captious reproaches.

WILL. Your past life hardly persuades me of your honor or your honesty.

EMILIA. I never claimed that merit, honor. How could a bastard Jewish girl be blessed with such a lofty English virtue?

WILL. I will not share your body.

EMILIA. Beware, beware of jealousy, Will. It is the green-eyed monster which doth mock the meat it feeds on.

WILL. "Green-eyed monster…mock the meat…" Hum, that could be something. Are you suggesting women lie to men because we cannot bear the truth?

EMILIA. Thou hast said it. And since you'd rather fight than love – and write than fight–I'll remove this offending object from your sight.

WILL. Doggerel.

*(***MARLOWE*** bursts into the room at this point, cheery as ever, but looking as if he had slept three nights in his clothes. He holds a flagon of Rhenish in his hand and downs it.)*

MARLOWE. How now, how now! How go maidenheads?

EMILIA. An accessory I haven't owned since first I came to court.

MARLOWE. The lass seems riggish. Alas, poor wretch, hast not slept tonight? Would he not, a naughty man, let it sleep?

WILL. 'Tis not the time for jesting, Kit.

MARLOWE. Ah, we've been quarreling, have we? Lover's broils are always preludes to amorous toils.

EMILIA. We have known each other not one week yet, and already the man would treat me as a piece of property.

MARLOWE. What each man spades, he thinks he owns. And our intrepid explorer has planted his flag in the New Atlantis.

EMILIA. The Queen commands this day that I make music for her. Goodbye Kit. Goodbye Will. And think well on what I told you.

WILL. Find the handkerchief!

(She leaves.)

MARLOWE. What handkerchief?

WILL. It's nothing, Kit. I barely know her yet, and still my heart is broke.

MARLOWE. Because of how you love. Putting pudendas on pedestals and prating about perfection.

WILL. Better that than pissing on pedestals and parroting Pyrrhonian pessimism.

MARLOWE. *(delighted)* Well done, Will! Shall we send the prurient paramour packing and alliterate together?

WILL. I cannot leave her, Kit. I cannot leave her or believe her.

MARLOWE. *Odi et amo*, Will, *odi et amo*. Didn't they teach you Catullus in your Stratford grammar school? You love and you hate.

WILL. Yes, her beauty I do love but hate I her dishonor.

MARLOWE. Tut, man, her honor is an essence that's not seen. They have it very oft that have it not.

WILL. You're such a cynic, Kit. No wonder you write such godless plays. But why so rumpled, man?

MARLOWE. I spent the night in prison. They yanked me out of bed and trundled me off to Newgate. Leaving Hal to captivate the watch.

WILL. For what cause? You've not been stealing purses again?

MARLOWE. Mistaken identity. I was released soon after. *(taking a leg of mutton off the table)* Was this your dinner?

WILL. *(nodding)* So Hal was in your bed?

MARLOWE. *(eating)* Of course. You didn't know? We have been boisterously banging bungholes this entire week.

WILL. I suspect he has known my mistress, too –

MARLOWE. Of course he has.

WILL. …served the lust of her heart –

MARLOWE. Voraciously…

WILL. …and done the act of darkness with her.

MARLOWE. When the fit is on him, the man is a centaur. Cocks, twats, cumquats, 'tis all the same to him.

WILL. And that is certain? He told you that?

MARLOWE. No, but last night I lay with him, and in his sleep he kissed me hard, and cried "Oh sweet Emilia." This mutton's good. I haven't supped since Wednesday.

WILL. Damnation!

MARLOWE. And then he laid his leg over my thigh, and sighed and stroked me, speaking her name.

WILL. The woman's a whore.

MARLOWE. No, no, the whore's a woman. You must allow the sex its foibles.

WILL. I do regret me now I ever left Stratford or betrayed my marriage bed.

MARLOWE. Why blame the lass, and not the lad?

WILL. Who? Hal?

MARLOWE. Yes, Hal. 'Tis no true sign of friendship to mount another's filly.

WILL. Those are petty wrongs that liberty commits.

MARLOWE. That libertines commit.

WILL. But he's still young.

MARLOWE. Mature enough to weave dark plots against the Queen. Do you want this mince pie?

WILL. What plots?

MARLOWE. Some madness he is hatching with that devil Essex. I know not the details. You desire revenge? Discover those plans to me.

WILL. I cannot, Kit. He is my patron. And my friend.

MARLOWE. And more than friend to me. *(his mouth full)* But still a traitor to the crown. *(He wipes his mouth with one of* **WILL** *'s sonnets.)*

WILL. Kit, you've barely left his bed, and you're planning to betray him?

MARLOWE. No, no, not Hal. Never Hal. I want his demon, that turncoat Essex. I'll keep our precious Harry free from harm.

WILL. That choice may not be yours. Why jeopardize his safety?

MARLOWE. I could say he hath a daily beauty in his life that makes me ugly. But I shan't because you'll say "Hum," and steal it.

WILL. Be serious, man. *(He is stealing it.)*

MARLOWE. *(desperate)* I have to give them something.

WILL. To earn your spy-keep? No.

MARLOWE. I need your aid in this. I'm asking you to trust me.

WILL. I cannot do that, Kit.

MARLOWE. Not for Queen and country?

WILL. Don't speak that rot to me.

MARLOWE. Not for queans and cuntery? Remember Hal betrayed you.

WILL. I'll not be false to one I love.

MARLOWE. Well then, I'll be gone. Clearly, a contented cuckold we have here.

WILL. *(stung)* I'll take my own action. I do not need to join Kit Marlowe's perfidies.

MARLOWE. Be they as prime as goats, as hot as monkeys, Will Shakespeare remains a cheerful witness. So long as he can make a poem. *(He leaves.)*

(**WILL** *returns to his table and starts to write. After doing a few lines, he throws the quill on the table in disgust.* **SOUTHAMPTON** *enters. He is wearing* **EMILIA***'s handkercief in his doublet.)*

SOUTHAMPTON. Was that our Kit I saw just now?

WILL. *(sullen)* Yes, my Lord.

SOUTHAMPTON. I thought he was in Newgate.

WILL. He was released.

SOUTHAMPTON. Of course he was. His friends are perched in elevated places.

WILL. He says he was detained in error.

SOUTHAMPTON. It was no error, Will. A spy called Baines informed on him to Cecil, saying the mouth of so dangerous a traitor should be stopped. They searched his rooms and found some atheist writings tacked up on the walls.

WILL. What writings?

SOUTHAMPTON. The usual heresies. Kit proudly gave me a copy of the ruffian's deposition:
Item: *"That the first beginning of religion was only to keep men in awe, and that all the New Testament is filthily written."*

WILL. The Gospel According to Saint Kit.

SOUTHAMPTON. Item: *"That if there be any God or any good religion, it is the Papists…and that all Protestants are hypocritical asses."* Well, he does show wisdom there.

WILL. He should have specified the Puritans. They are the true hypocrites.

SOUTHAMPTON. Item: *"That the sacrament would have been much better instituted in a tobacco pipe."*

WILL. That's Kit, all right. But if proven his, these words will be his passport to a gallows on Tyburn hill.

SOUTHAMPTON. I have often heard him say as much.

WILL. He drew his Mephistophelis in his own dark blood. How did he secure his release?

SOUTHAMPTON. Even now, his chamber mate, Thom Kyd, is being racked and thumb-screwed to confess the crime.

WILL. They are torturing Thom Kyd? I know him as a firm believer in the English Church.

SOUTHAMPTON. Kyd says the writings belong to Marlowe, Marlowe says they belong to Kyd. Lord Cecil is more willing to believe the spy in his employ than the wretch upon the rack.

WILL. Poor Kyd. He is his own Spanish Tragedy.

SOUTHAMPTON. Marlowe would sacrifice his sainted grandmother to save his own precious skin. He is a dangerous pard when cornered.

WILL. Kit was well prepared to sacrifice you for being in league with Essex in some conspiracy against the crown.

SOUTHAMPTON. He knew that, did he? His spying eyes are everywhere.

WILL. What are you planning? Can you confide in me?

SOUTHAMPTON. I have come here for that purpose. But first, you must swear upon my sword to maintain secrecy.

WILL. You have all my fealty, love.

SOUTHAMPTON. Nay, but swear. I need an oath as well.

WILL. I swear by all that's holy to keep your secrets safe.

SOUTHAMPTON. Keep faith with all that's holy. I need your hand in this.

WILL. What is afoot?

SOUTHAMPTON. A mighty enterprise beginning with a raid upon the Exchequer. My guardian Burleigh, the Treasurer to the Crown, would rob my inheritance from me. 'Tis meet I steal the Queen's inheritance from him. It will finance our adventure.

WILL. What adventure?

SOUTHAMPTON. Are you prepared for wonders?

WILL. I am so.

SOUTHAMPTON. And will be close?

WILL. As the grave.

SOUTHAMPTON. We plan to march into the Queen's own chambers and hold the wrinkled crone fast prisoner.

WILL. (*frightened*) For what purpose, Lord?

SOUTHAMPTON. She must agree to put aside her crown and invest Scotland's James Stuart as Albion's true King.

WILL. I am shocked, my loved lord. I know not what to say.

SOUTHAMPTON. That's good. Then you'll say nothing.

WILL. Depose the Queen?

SOUTHAMPTON. And hold her in the Tower.

WILL. I fear this will be the end of you. And if of you, of me.

SOUTHAMPTON. You'll soon be writing celebratory odes to a new sovereign, Scottish King Jamie.

WILL. But James was raised a Protestant.

SOUTHAMPTON. He is the son of Catholic Mary.

WILL. And should the Queen refuse to abdicate?

SOUTHAMPTON. Then we will send the loathsome tyrant hurtling down to hell.

WILL. I am amazed, my Lord, and greatly afeard. What you speak is treason. You will lose your head.

SOUTHAMPTON. 'Tis sometimes necessary to lance a sickly canker to restore the health of the commonwealth. Essex has gathered fifty English nobles to his cause, and all do hate the Queen. The rabblement will be bought off with the hag's own crowns. The question now is this: Will you keep these sealéd documents in your possession?

WILL. Why here?

SOUTHAMPTON. There is no reason to suspect a poet.

WILL. There is every reason to suspect a poet indebted to a Catholic patron.

SOUTHAMPTON. A debt I ask you now in part to pay.

WILL. Can you inform me of the content of these papers, loved Lord?

SOUTHAMPTON. Should I do that, you will be implicated.

WILL. I am implicate already.

SOUTHAMPTON. Descriptions of our plans and a detailed map of the Exchequer.

WILL. I am afeared, my love.

SOUTHAMPTON. You have received much bounty at my hands. I ask a little back.

WILL. I have received much bounty–and some injury as well.

SOUTHAMPTON. What injury is that?

WILL. *(hands him a sonnet)* Here.

SOUTHAMPTON. Is this a time for poetry?

WILL. Read it, please.

SOUTHAMPTON. *(reading)* "Two loves have I, a bright one and a dark…. my female evil tempteth my better angel from my side." These are metaphors. Be more precise.

WILL. All right, in plain downright English, I fear Emilia has enticed you to her bed, and know not which of you to mourn the most…

SOUTHAMPTON. Now hush, and let your brighter angel speak. 'Tis true I have topped the fair Emilia. And true it is that she hath tempted me.

WILL. Ay me! I would the whole court had tasted her sweet body had I not known it.

SOUTHAMPTON. But, Will, I never thought you did regard the woman as other than a sometime bedfellow….

WILL. And so I did until I saw my handkerchief in your hand.

SOUTHAMPTON. Oh, this napkin's yours? Then have it back again. *(taking it from his doublet)* And the black-haired wench to boot. Your fault is too much faith in women. I ne'er did trust the sex since first my mother did deceive my father, and with her priest confessor.

WILL. Your mother faithless with a priest?

SOUTHAMPTON. When I was six. My Dad did drive her from the house forthwith, while I did drench the parting scene with tears. From that time hence I have looked to men alone for trust and loyalty.

WILL. And you have mine. My heart is sore, but never do I blame you, Lord. Take all my loves, my love, yea, take them all. Your fault is youth, not wantonness.

SOUTHAMPTON. What's that?!!

WILL. I do not mean to chide.

SOUTHAMPTON. And shall not. Remember you your place.

WILL. I do, I do. Let us still be friends. If I lose you, then I lose that which leaves me most bereft. Give me the papers. *(puts them in a wardrobe)* I shall keep them in my cupboard locked, and this key shall be my close companion. *(puts it around his neck)*

SOUTHAMPTON. Will Shakespeare, you are a steady anchor in a heavy sea of calumny. But I am very sorry that with Emilia I forgot myself.

WILL. There is no need for self-reproof. And that my love may appear most plain and free, all that is mine in Emilia I give to thee.

SOUTHAMPTON. 'Tis gracious of you, Will, but I shall see her face no more.

WILL. No more will I. *(grimly)* If I can shake the faithless wanton from my heart.

SOUTHAMPTON. Then farewell, Will. And wish our venture bon voyage.

WILL. I pray God guide you safely to the shore.

*(**SOUTHAMPTON** hugs **WILL** in a long embrace which **WILL**, after a hesitant moment, returns. **SOUTHAMPTON** looks deeply into his face.)*

SOUTHAMPTON. This is affection, not condescension, Will.

WILL. I know that, my loved Lord.

SOUTHAMPTON. Come with me now. I know your love for me is not the carnal kind, nor mine for you. I need your friendship, and the comfort of your voice and verse.

WILL. My service is yours, my Lord. And all my faith is yours. Your love is greater than high birth to me.

*(They leave arm in arm. The lights dim. A moment passes. **MARLOWE** enters, reeling drunk. He proceeds to ransack the room. Sees the closet, jimmies it open, finds **SOUTHAMPTON**'s sealed documents, opens the seal, reads, reseals, and puts them in his pocket. Sits in **WILL**'s chair – and weeps.)*

ACT IV

(The same. A few days later. **EMILIA** *is sitting in* **WILL** *'s chair, reading through his sonnets.* **WILL** *enters through the door.)*

WILL. It's you.

EMILIA. Yes, your faithless lover.

WILL. Thou hast said it.

EMILIA. I have come to return remembrances of yours.

WILL. I never gave you aught.

EMILIA. You know right well you did.

WILL. Are you faithful?

EMILIA. In my fashion.

WILL. The fashion of women who cannot live both honest and fair.

EMILIA. Those words are too subtle for me, Will Shakespeare. But since you arraign me with dishonesty, let me return the charge on you.

WILL. How so?

EMILIA. Have you not likewise left a marriage couch to dishonor yourself in mine?

WILL. 'Tis true I have deprived another bed's revenue of its rent. In loving thee I do betray a lawful wife. But you are twice forsworn.

EMILIA. How so?

WILL. In loving me, you broke your marriage-vow. In loving Hal, you broke a vow to me, and made your womb a cistern for foul toads to knot and gender in.

EMILIA. You men, you men. Forever slandering our sex when yours is far more faithless. And much more blameworthy. For when we bear your weight do not we also bear the burdens of that weight?

WILL. *(startled)* What burdens?

EMILIA. I think I am with child.

WILL. That's news. And who's the happy father?

EMILIA. Who else but you? *(She slaps his face.)*

WILL. *(He slaps her back, a slap on every name.)* Who else, but Tom and Dick and Harry Wriothesley and no doubt ten score bedmates.

EMILIA. *(heading for the door)* You are the only begetter.

WILL. We'll never know for certain, will we?

EMILIA. Well, know for certain this child I carry shall never bear your name or name you father. Or be in ear-shot when you vilify its mother.

WILL. And now we talk of amorous burdens, let me name what I do carry.

EMILIA. What?

WILL. A fever, longing still for that which longer nurseth the disease.

EMILIA. You mean your appetite for me.

WILL. I mean a canker of my appetite for you.

EMILIA. Not the plague!!

WILL. No, the pox, the French disease, the plague of lovers, customers, and gulls.

EMILIA. But are you sure?

WILL. Sure and past cure. For I have sworn thee fair, and thought thee bright, who art as black as hell, as dark as night.

EMILIA. Will, I can listen no longer. The only way I serve you is to deepen your scorn of womankind. A hateful function for a lover.

WILL. Swear to me you're true, and I'll force myself to believe it.

EMILIA. True, false. Why make you one small part of us the sum of your affection, and one brief act our chief value and utility? What is a woman's body to you? A sacred vessel polluted by the merest hint of frailty? Why do you embrace your vile suspicions more ardently than you hold our loves?

WILL. Because it is a carnal planet. And strumpets will say anything.

EMILIA. You talk of purity when you mean possession. Wives and mistresses are but property.

WILL. Infected property.

EMILIA. I have loved you for a poet and a man. Ignored your weaknesses, admired your strengths. Tried to be an equal partner by your side. But all you wanted was a loyal lapdog licking its master's hand.

WILL. Better than a bawdy belwether cuckolding a credulous ram.

(grabbing her shoulders) Name me all your lovers.

EMILIA. Why, so you can sermonize still more about my soiléd soul?

WILL. You have been with many men.

EMILIA. And does that corrupt me in your eyes?

WILL. In my eyes, and those of all mankind.

EMILIA. The argument is bootless. I will no more of it. Goodbye, Will Shakespeare.

WILL. *(grabbing her by the arm)* You will not leave here till I say you leave.

EMILIA. Let go of me.

WILL. *(throws her on the bed)* Nay, stay, and sit you down; you shall not budge.

EMILIA. What will you do? You will not injure me?

WILL. Have you prayed tonight, Emilia?

EMILIA. Don't be a jackass. Get off my bones.

(She does a stunning flip that tosses him off the bed and onto the floor.)

WILL. 'Tis just as well. I have no appetite for this revenge.

EMILIA. Nor yet the heart nor courage. Yes, you can imagine such a man, maddened by jealousy, driven to cruelty, but not inhabit him. 'Tis strange that one so strong creating persons of the drama should struggle so to find himself.

WILL. Because I cannot be a murderer?

EMILIA. Because you cannot be a man.

WILL. Not a man? I?

EMILIA. If being a man means wedding thought to action, then marry your manhood – mew!

WILL. So in order to prove myself manly, I must murder you.

EMILIA. I do not think you have the stomach for it.

(WILL *takes a pillow as if to put it over her face, then drops the pillow.*)

WILL. You are right. I am not the hero of my own revenge play, only a secondary player, an attendant lord. A cipher, a neuter, a man without a will.

EMILIA. In brief, a playwright.

WILL. A playwright, yes. For whom you have contempt.

EMILIA. Never for the playwright. Him I will always admire. Your wealth of wit, your way with words, would conquer any woman's heart. But if the man were half the measure of his muse, ah me, what might have been.

WILL. Ah me, what might have been.

(*They sit in silence for a moment.*)

So, girl, where do we find ourselves?

EMILIA. You find me here. But now 'tis meet we part. I will home to mourn our short-lived love, and harden my heart against the future hurts of men. Farewell, Will.

WILL. Farewell, Emilia. Take back your instrument. (*offering her the recorder*)

EMILIA. Nay, keep it as a relic of our passing love.

WILL. And you can keep my handkerchief. The artifact of my broken trust.

EMILIA. If I've failed you as a Muse, Will, then confess I've served you as a model.

WILL. For what?

EMILIA. For all your faithless females.

WILL. You will no doubt inspire an infinite variety of heroines.

EMILIA. Thank you, Will. Then not all is lost.

(She leaves. WILL takes the recorder and tries to play a few notes, but gives up. Enter SOUTHAMPTON, carrying some leaflets.)

SOUTHAMPTON. I saw your Jewess passing on the stairs.

WILL. No longer mine. The bond is cut.

SOUTHAMPTON. Be comforted. Young as I am, I know that love is fleeting.

WILL. I will survive this. But I fear that something precious has vanished from my life.

SOUTHAMPTON. There will be other loves.

WILL. I hope not. God, I hope not. How goes your enterprise?

SOUTHAMPTON. How but ill. Have you examined your cupboard lately?

WILL. Why no. *(He sees it has been jimmied open.)* Alas, they have discovered me.

SOUTHAMPTON. Say rather *he* – who has discovered *me!*

WILL. Which he?

SOUTHAMPTON. Marlowe.

WILL. Marlowe has the papers? We are lost.

SOUTHAMPTON. No, Marlowe is lost. I have prepared a snare for him to trap his treacherous soul.

WILL. What trap?

SOUTHAMPTON. These verses, forged after Kit's own hand and signed with the name of "Tamburlaine." They have been posted on the walls of the Dutch Church.

WILL. Verses are not treasons.

SOUTHAMPTON. These are. A list of indictments libelling the Dutch religion.

WILL. That's but a trifling wrong.

SOUTHAMPTON. Not when the malformed Cecil is trading with the Dutch and needs their friendship. But here's the thing assured to send a shiver through the crookback's hump. His favorite informer is a double agent for the King of Spain.

WILL. Truly? Kit is intemperate and rash, but yet a loyal Englishman.

SOUTHAMPTON. Loyal to all sides and to none. Plutus is his god, for where the gold is there is Marlowe. Did you know he was arrested in the Lowlands once for counterfeiting gold coins?

WILL. *(incredulous)* No.

SOUTHAMPTON. It is mentioned in the Baines deposition. Item: *"I have as good a right to coin as the Queen of England."* That sentiment will not endear him to the tightfisted witch.

WILL. There is much I do not know about Kit Marlowe. He is a man of masks.

SOUTHAMPTON. And one of them, the mask of a Spanish spy.

WILL. How know you this?

SOUTHAMPTON. Why, man, he told me so himself. Thinking I would favor any Papist monarch rather than the Queen, he showed me a letter confirming him in the pay of the King of Spain.

WILL. And this is the greatest poet in England?

SOUTHAMPTON. His rhyming days are over. He goes now to a long imprisonment.

WILL. For slandering the Dutch?

SOUTHAMPTON. For pandering the Spanish. My plans he stole from you I stole back from him, and exchanged them with the incriminating letter I purloined from his chamber.

WILL. So you recovered the documents he stole from you.

SOUTHAMPTON. Yes, here they are, still carrying mine own broken seal. *(He removes it from his doublet.)* And having a signet in my purse, I set a new seal on his Spanish letter and placed it in his cabinet. Kit will deliver himself to Sir Robert Cecil, thinking he is delivering me. What Marlowe would use as proof of my vile treason, will now prove evidence of his own.

WILL. So Kit goes to the Tower.

SOUTHAMPTON. Why, man, he did make love to this employment. He is not near my conscience. But we must find some safer place to hide these papers. Now that I've been named, the Queen's keen eyes are everywhere.

WILL. Give them me.

SOUTHAMPTON. Your cupboard has already proved unsafe.

WILL. *(removing the mouthpiece from the recorder)* But not this harmless instrument. It is a hiding place the Watch will never search.

SOUTHAMPTON. Unless possessed by a sudden whim to hear a chorus of "Greensleeves"?

WILL. Let us pray they have no ear for song. Come sir, put on this costume and take you this lute. You are now a strolling musician. The disguise will help you home unnoticed.

SOUTHAMPTON. A player at last. Then there's still a hope I may some day become a player king.

WILL. *(helping him with his costume)* As for that, my loving Lord, I beg you think no more on this rebellion. Your escape has been exceeding narrow.

SOUTHAMPTON. No more, it's over.

WILL. Thank God.

SOUTHAMPTON. Postponed, not ended, till a better time.

WILL. I say burn the wretched papers and think no more upon it.

(**MARLOWE** *enters, looking even more wasted than ever. He is quite drunk and carrying a bottle of sherris-sack.*)

MARLOWE. You here, Hal? Why this strange apparel? I thought by now you'd be half across the channel on your way to France. Dangerous times to be abroad.

SOUTHAMPTON. You make them dangerous.

MARLOWE. I know not what you mean.

SOUTHAMPTON. Don't play the innocent with me. I know you would discover our design to the Secretary of State.

MARLOWE. To Cecil? *(Pause. Hard look.)* I would and did. Me duty as a loyal subject of the Crown.

SOUTHAMPTON. Don't use that cant with me.

MARLOWE. What cant? A villainous asp would bite the teat of our most virtuous Queen. 'Tis just we stamp the serpent under foot. Even now, the headsman is sharpening an axe inscribéd with the name of Robert Devereux, second Earl of Essex.

SOUTHAMPTON. And a second with the name of Henry Wriothesley, third Earl of Southampton.

MARLOWE. No, dear Hal, your name was never at issue. But it would not be amiss if you, so close in friendship to the traitor Essex, could spend some leisure months across the channel fondling local garcons.

SOUTHAMPTON. You would drive me into exile? And still you dare to face me here? Have you no fear of my naked weapon? *(He draws his sword.)*

MARLOWE. I have seen your naked weapon. And oft been penetrated by the fearsome tool.

WILL. This is no time for jesting, Kit.

SOUTHAMPTON. Your blood is not worth the letting. You are a scoundrel and a knave.

MARLOWE. (**MARLOWE** *draws his sword and dagger.*) I will not take that, even from you, boy!

SOUTHAMPTON. Boy! I am twice the man that you are.

WILL. Gentlemen, gentlemen. Put up your swords.

SOUTHAMPTON. I am half-inclined to beat you from these quarters.

MARLOWE. Beat me? I am not your drum.

SOUTHAMPTON. No, you are my flute, and I will pipe you down to hell.

MARLOWE. And this is how you show your gratitude?

SOUTHAMPTON. Gratitude for betraying me?

MARLOWE. No, for saving you. Did you not read my letter?

SOUTHAMPTON. I have received no messages from you.

MARLOWE. Oh, oh, quite right, quite right. *(feeling in his pockets)*
I was too insensible to deliver same. Well, here it is. "Fly London. Your life's at risk. The Queen knows all." A little late, a bit declarative, too terse, bare imagery, but the meaning's clear enough. You still have time.

SOUTHAMPTON. It is you who should fly London, your life that stands at risk.

MARLOWE. Me? A close favorite of the Queen, under the protection of her shriveled right arm, Lord Cecil? Everybody at court loves Kit Marlowe.

SOUTHAMPTON. I doubt the beloved Kit Marlowe will ever find favor at the court again.

MARLOWE. No? Then why would Cecil send me to Deptford on secret matters of state? I'd call that favor, wouldn't you?

WILL. Perhaps he feels your pickled brain needs exposure to the salt sea air.

SOUTHAMPTON. There is no sea air in a tavern.

MARLOWE. I go not to a tavern, but to the home of Eleanor Bull, a hostess with the best-stocked cellar in the shire. *(to* WILL*)* What is that bawdy object hanging by your neck?

SOUTHAMPTON. An object that would hang me by my neck, did you know its contents.

MARLOWE. What say you?

WILL. An alto recorder.

MARLOWE. I love the instrument. Do you know "Greensleeves"?

(WILL *gives a look at* HAL.)

SOUTHAMPTON. Kit, adieu. I do not think that we shall meet again.

MARLOWE. We shall meet, and once again be friends, when this broil dies down and you return from France.

SOUTHAMPTON. Kit.

MARLOWE. Yes?

SOUTHAMPTON. What was it Mephistophelis replied when Faustus asked him how he had escaped from hell?

MARLOWE. "Why this is hell, nor am I out of it."

SOUTHAMPTON. Think on it.

MARLOWE. I think on it every day.

SOUTHAMPTON. And comb your hair. Such laggardly looks do ill become a poet and a scholar. *(He leaves.)*

WILL. There was a time I envied no man more than you.

MARLOWE. Keep your quills sharpened, Shakespeare. You will be a great poet some day. Perhaps the best in England once Kit Marlowe leaves this earth. But whom will you steal from then?

(WILL *leaves. The lights fade.* MARLOWE *sits on the bed. Takes a long swig, finishes the bottle, and throws it out of the window)*

MARLOWE. *(calling)* Francis. Francis! FRANCIS!!!! *(no answer)* Welcome to hell.

(lies down)

(blackout)

ACT V

(WILL is alone in his room writing. The melancholy sound of a recorder air accompanies him at his labors. The lights come up further to reveal EMILIA in the door, a book in her hand.)

WILL. "When, in disgrace with fortune and men's eyes,
    I all alone beweep my outcast state
    And trouble deaf heaven with my bootless cries
    And look upon myself and curse my fate,
    Wishing me like to one more rich in hope,
    Featured like him, like him with friends possess'd,
    Desiring this man's art and that man's scope,
    With what I most enjoy contented least;
    Yet in these thoughts myself almost despising,
    Haply I think on thee, and then my state,
    Like to the lark at break of day arising
    From sullen earth, sings hymns at heaven's gate;
    For thy sweet love remember'd such wealth brings
    That then I scorn to change my state with kings."

EMILIA. Very elegant, Will, and very eloquent. I am certain Hal will be very touched to find himself memorialized thus.

WILL. Why are you here? I thought we put full stop to our story when last we met.

EMILIA. I come to bring you news. Bad news.

WILL. *(frightened)* Hal is dead.

EMILIA. No, Marlowe.

WILL. What?!!!

EMILIA. Killed in Deptford.

WILL. And do you know the circumstances?

EMILIA. All that I know is that following some quarrel over a bill, Marlowe was stabbed to death like a common brawler.

WILL. Kit never quarreled over bills. He never paid them.

EMILIA. And that he died aswearing.

WILL. "Tongue curse thy fill and die."

(**EMILIA** *looks quizzically at him.*)

The last words of Kit's Jew, Barabas.

(**SOUTHAMPTON** *comes bursting into the room at this point, very flustered.*)

SOUTHAMPTON. Have you heard?

WILL. Emilia just told me.

SOUTHAMPTON. Dead.

WILL. Do you know any more of the matter?

SOUTHAMPTON. I have the coroner's report. The Queen has distributed it throughout the court.

EMILIA. Wherefore?

SOUTHAMPTON. I assume our gracious majesty would like to quash the slightest presumption of foul play.

WILL. What do you think?

SOUTHAMPTON. Murder most foul, though the murderer be free.

WILL. His name?

SOUTHAMPTON. Ingram Frizer.

EMILIA. I know the man. A moneylender, and a spy in the employ of Robert Cecil.

SOUTHAMPTON. Then we can guess who put him to it.

WILL. How did he die?

SOUTHAMPTON. According to the coroner, a worthy named William Danby, three men were drinking with Kit in a safe house owned by Eleanor Bull of Deptford. They dined and passed the time, walked in the garden, returned to the room, and ate till six. There was an argument over the pence, or "le grand recknynge," as the coroner called it, displaying his impeccable French. The report further affirms that Marlowe, lying on a bed, of a sudden drew Frizer's dagger and attacked him from behind, lacerating his face. Recovering his weapon, Frizir plunged it into Marlowe's eye, making a wound two inches deep and one inch wide, entering the brain and killing him instantly.

WILL. A great reckoning in a little room. The coward conquest of a wretch's knife.

EMILIA. Well, the coroner is exact, at least, about the dimensions of the wound.

SOUTHAMPTON. And the cost of the dagger–twelve pence.

WILL. The knave is nothing if not absolute.

SOUTHAMPTON. But not about his name. The coroner writes him down as Christopher Morley.

WILL. I wonder if they'll mangle my surname, too, the day I vanish from this life?

EMILIA. Not if you ever spell it consistently. I have some seven different autographs in your hand.

WILL. And where is Master Morley buried?

SOUTHAMPTON. Nobody knows. They pitched his body in an unmarked grave.

WILL. Something is rotten in this story.

SOUTHAMPTON. And something hurried, too. Frizer was held but thirty-six hours and then released, on a plea of self-defense.

WILL. And so the life of the foremost poet in the world is snuffed out like a penny candle, extinguished with half his music in him.

SOUTHAMPTON. We have his plays. They are yet his monument.

EMILIA. Why do men need monuments? Is not a fully-lived life enough?

WILL. All men need something to shield them from mortality.

EMILIA. I have that something in my belly–the surest bridge to the next life. It could be yours as well.

WILL. I already have three children, and one of them lies ill. The flesh is mortal. Art is not.

EMILIA. But this child could have been the harvest of our love.

WILL. The only certain harvest of our love is the canker in my groin. I know who gave me that. But no man can truly know he is the father of his child.

EMILIA. I fear we are in for another sonnet sequence on the subject of female inconstancy. And so I'll take my leave. Oh, before I forget. I came to give you a copy of a book of poems of mine that has been newly pressed.

WILL. You have written this?

EMILIA. Yes. The first collection of poetry published by a woman in England.

WILL. I'll wager I know the subject of it.

EMILIA. Yes, verses on the female sex, and the slanderers who'd impugn it.

WILL. Meaning me.

EMILIA. Meaning you and Hal and Kit and all the men I've known. At last, we are telling our side of the story.

WILL. I will read these poems with interest.

EMILIA. Even though the rhymes are doggerel?

WILL. I shall treat them with the respect them deserve.

EMILIA. Much better, Will. Treat everything as deserved, and what will escape censure? I go. But first let us take hands in a circle and remember that wretched remnant, that piece of dust called Christopher Marlowe.

(The three take hands and form a circle for a moment of silence.)

SOUTHAMPTON. I feel his tortured spirit with us here.

EMILIA. Perhaps it will find rest in the hearts of his one-time friends. Farewell to the love that might have been.

*(She kisses **WILL**.)*

And farewell to the shadow that came between.

*(She brushes past **HAL** and leaves.)*

SOUTHAMPTON. *(after a pause)* I murdered him.

WILL. He was a man quite destined for disaster. If it had not happened now, yet it would have come. The question was the when.

SOUTHAMPTON. He would still be here, ale pot in hand, cursing God with a merry sneer, had I not switched the documents.

WILL. And had you not switched them, perhaps it would be you lying prostrate in an unmarked grave.

SOUTHAMPTON. Which urges me to leave this land. I will heed Marlowe's advice and take a packet boat for France, before the Queen do turn her fury full on me. Will, here is a purse to help you finish your sonnets – enough there, I expect, to buy a full share in your company.

WILL. My Lord, I am speechless with gratitude. But how will I continue without you?

SOUTHAMPTON. You have your poetry.

WILL. But not the inspiration for that poetry. Once these sonnets are completed, my career as a poet will be over, too.

SOUTHAMPTON. What will you do?

WILL. Write plays. Emilia said I knew not who I was, and she was right. A poet is the subject of his own work. A playwright is invisible, existing through the people of his invention. I am fit only to create the lives of others.

SOUTHAMPTON. And what are you planning for your next dramatic work?

WILL. I want to conclude my Henry cycle, with a play on the rule of Richard the Third.

SOUTHAMPTON. Like Cecil, an evil crookback in the court.

WILL. Deep in the winter of his discontent.

SOUTHAMPTON. Goodbye, sweet Will.

WILL. Goodbye, my loving Lord.

(A long embrace. SOUTHAMPTON *leaves.* WILL *goes back to his desk.)*

WILL. *(soliloquizing)* My Muse is dead, my lord is fled, my mistress sped, and I am here alone. Weary with day I long for endless night, a sleep that has no waking, a place of existence and extinction. To be or not to be…

(WILL *sits musing as the lights come slowly up on* MARLOWE*'s ghost, standing in the shadows. He gives three short loud claps of his hands.)*

WILL. Kit!!!

MARLOWE'S GHOST. That's a nice start for a tragic soliloquy. The hero contemplating his own suicide in rough draft.

WILL. We thought you dead.

MARLOWE'S GHOST. I am dead.

(He comes out of the shadows, pale, his right eye bloodied, as in the Prologue.)

Don't I make a fearsome ghost?

WILL. There are no ghosts except in playhouses.

MARLOWE'S GHOST. The exception stands before you.

WILL. The hairs are standing on my neck.

MARLOWE'S GHOST. Don't tremble. A ghost has no more substance than a thought. And you will surely find some way to use me in your plays.

WILL. You were stabbed in the eye at Deptford.

MARLOWE'S GHOST. The eye that squinnies at you now.

WILL. A brawl.

MARLOWE'S GHOST. An assassination ordered by the Queen.

WILL. As we suspected.

MARLOWE'S GHOST. No doubt my just dessert. But, oh how I miss the strong potations at the Mermaid.

WILL. What would you have me do? Avenge your foul and most unnatural murder?

MARLOWE'S GHOST. No, complete my short and fragmentary career. You have always walked in my footsteps. Now be my footsteps.

WILL. I do not well understand you.

MARLOWE'S GHOST. I died with more than thirty plays and scores of people birthing in my brain. You must be their midwife.

WILL. You want me to channel your unfinished work?

MARLOWE'S GHOST. And make of it your own.

WILL. *(excited)* What type of plays? What kind of people?

MARLOWE'S GHOST. A pair of star-crossed lovers, separated by their families. A romantic tragedy.

(**WILL** *should speak these lines, as if in a trance.*)

JULIET. "Oh happy dagger. This is thy sheath."

ROMEO. "Thus with a kiss I die."

MARLOWE'S GHOST. A lively lady who dons doublet and hose to pursue her lover into the forest of Arden. A pastoral romance.

ROSALIND. "Men have died from time to time, and worms have eaten them, but not for love."

MARLOWE'S GHOST. A fat and witty coward knight discarded by the prince that he loves. A chronicle of cutpurses and kings.

FALSTAFF. "God save thy grace, King Hal! my royal Hal!… God save thee, my sweet boy!"

MARLOWE'S GHOST. A melancholy prince sworn to avenge his murdered father, hesitant and irresolute like his author. A tragedy of blood.

HAMLET. "How all occasions do inform against me, and spur my dull revenge."

MARLOWE'S GHOST. A Moorish general who smothers his beloved wife, because some villain has impeached her loyalty. A domestic tragedy and much ado about a handkerchief.

OTHELLO. "Put out the light, and then put out the light."

MARLOWE'S GHOST. A peerless Egyptian queen undone by passion for her Roman general. A love tragedy whose spirited heroine is not unlike Emilia.

CLEOPATRA. "Give me my robe, put on my crown; I have Immortal longings in me."

MARLOWE'S GHOST. An aged king who plunges into wisdom through an abyss of suffering.

KING LEAR. "Thou'lt come no more. Never, never, never, never, never!"

MARLOWE'S GHOST. And a magician on an enchanted isle who bids farewell to his charmèd art. A metaphysical romance and your goodbye to writing plays.

PROSPERO. "And deeper than did ever plummet sound I'll drown my book."

MARLOWE. Hum! Now that will be something!

WILL. *(hungry for more)* And would that be the last?

MARLOWE'S GHOST. The last before you return to Stratford and an abandoned wife, where every third thought shall be your grave.

WILL. And my reward?

MARLOWE'S GHOST. Immortality.

WILL. It is the bargain Faustus struck with Mephistophelis.

MARLOWE'S GHOST. That bargain I did make myself, and hourly repent me for it. No, I ask not for your soul, but your uncommon spirit.

WILL. And where will you be then?

MARLOWE'S GHOST. A shadow by your side, an echo in your ear, Bequeathing you a legacy of two great plays a year. The secret source of stories that make up the design, The wellspring of your faculty to never blot a line.

WILL. Be easy. I will do it.

MARLOWE'S GHOST. Then Will, take up thy quill. *(agonized tone)* My hour is almost come when I to sulphurous and tormenting flames must render up myself. Remember me. *(old mischievous self)* You are at liberty to use those lines.

WILL. Alas, poor ghost. Rest, rest, perturbed spirit.

MARLOWE'S GHOST. And those lines, too.

WILL. Vanished! An apparition? Or a figment of my fevered brain. No matter. He's left me stories in my head enough to last me twenty years. The star-crossed lovers united in death, let's start with that. *(writing)* "Two households, both alike in dignity...."

MARLOWE'S GHOST. *(voice over, hollow and profound)* Exit Ghost.

WILL. "In fair Verona where we lay our scene...." *(He trails off, and continues writing.)*

MARLOWE'S GHOST. *(fading away)* Enter William Shakespeare.

(blackout)

End of Play